# God is within me!

# God is within me!

# God is within me!

# God is within me!

# God is within me!

# God is within me!

# God is within me!

# God is within me!

# God is within me!

# God is within me!

God is within me!

# God is within me!

# God is within me!

# God is within me!

# God is within me!

# God is within me!

God is within me!

# God is within me!

# God is within me!

# God is within me!

# God is within me!

# God is within me!

God is within me!

# God is within me!

# God is within me!

# God is within me!

# God is within me!

# God is within me!

# God is within me!

# God is within me!

God is within me!

# God is within me!

# God is within me!

# God is within me!

# God is within me!

www.ingramcontent.com/pod-product-compliance
Lightning Source LLC
LaVergne TN
LVHW051923060526
838201LV00060B/4145